NUTS
from Forest, Orchard, and Field

Books by Gray Johnson Poole

NUTS FROM FOREST, ORCHARD, AND FIELD
ARCHITECTS AND MAN'S SKYLINE

Books by Lynn and Gray Poole

DEEP IN CAVES AND CAVERNS
SCIENTISTS WHO WORK OUTDOORS
INSECT-EATING PLANTS
FIREFLIES IN NATURE AND THE LABORATORY
VOLCANOES IN ACTION
DANGER! ICEBERGS AHEAD!

NUTS
from Forest, Orchard, and Field

GRAY JOHNSON POOLE

ILLUSTRATED WITH PHOTOGRAPHS

Dodd, Mead & Company · New York

Photographs are courtesy of the following: Agricultural Extension, University of California: page 19. California Almond Growers Exchange: page 43. Castle & Cooke Foods: pages 46, 48. Dr. Julian C. Crane: page 31. Diamond Walnut Growers: page 54. Dr. Dale E. Kester: page 41. Oregon Filbert Commission: pages 69, 70, 71. United States Department of Agriculture: pages 12, 15, 28, 29, 36, 53, 56, 61, 62, 64, 65, 75, 76, 81, 82, 85, 89.

ISBN: 0-396-06993-2
Library of Congress Catalog Card Number: 74-7662
Printed in the United States of America

This book is for
the Hawleys:
Renée and Dick
Michelle and Richie

ACKNOWLEDGMENTS

My sincere appreciation goes to the following who provided me with information and materials for this book:

American Pharmaceutical Association: Dr. William S. Apple, Executive Director, and George G. Griffenhagen, Associate Executive Director for Communications

The Connecticut Agricultural Experiment Station: Dr. Richard A. Jaynes, Associate Geneticist

California Almond Growers Exchange: Rupert Wrangham, Secretary-Treasurer, and Jeff P. Marx, Editor *Almond Facts*

General Foods Corporation

Diamond Walnut Growers: Donald L. Watson, Field Manager

W. D. Fowler and Sons, Corporation: Glen Fowler, Vice-President, and Mark Pepple, Horticulturist

Laura Scudder's, Snack Food Division, PET, B.J. Marshall, Consumer Services

United States Department of Agriculture: Office of Communication, Photography Division, Ms. Ruth Price; Northeastern Forest Experiment Station, Forest Service, Russell S. Walters, Research Forester; Agricultural Research Service, Plant Science Research, Department of Horticulture, Oregon State University, H. B. Lagerstedt, Research Horticulturist; Agricultural Research Service, Northeastern Research Region, Agricultural Research Center, Wallace K. Bailey, Research Horticulturist

National Peanut Council, Ms. Virginia Blair, Public Relations

Peanut Butter Manufacturers and Nut Salters Association, James E. Mack, Managing Director and General Counsel

Professor J.H. Mitchell, Jr., Clemson University, College of Agricultural Sciences, Department of Food Science

Theodore R. Sills, Inc., John C. Bohan, Vice-President

Brazilian Embassy, Washington, D.C., Sergio de Queiroz Duarte, Counselor, Press Office

General Foods Corporation, Public Relations Library

Oregon Filbert Commission, D.J. Duncan, Executive Secretary

University of California, Parlier, California: Agricultural Extension, Karl W. Opitz, Extension Subtropical Horticulturist

University of California at Davis: Dr. Julian C. Crane, Professor of Pomology; Dr. Dale E. Kester, Professor and Pomologist

Castle & Cooke Foods, W.M. Hale, Director, Specialty Food Products

California Macadamia Society, Ms. Mae N. Hornum, Secretary-Treasurer

Standard Brands Foods, Ms. Mary Lynn Woods, Consumer Service Department

Florida Cooperative Extension Service, University of Florida, Institute of Food and Agricultural Sciences, Timothy E. Crocker, Assistant Horticulturist

Madame Wu's Garden, Santa Monica, Cal., James Wong

Rabbi Albert Lewis, Los Angeles

Dr. Abraham Zygielbaum, Professor, Hebrew Union College, Los Angeles

Ms. Serenna Day, Children's Librarian, Brentwood Library, Los Angeles

Photographs came from many sources as the credits indicate. Special thanks are offered to Ms. Ruth Price, Photography Division, Office of Communication, United States Department of Agriculture, who searched diligently and cheerfully for specific pictures required for illustration.

I am grateful to Glen Fowler, Vice-President, and Mark Pepple, Horticulturist, of W.D. Fowler and Sons, Corporation, who gave so generously of their time when I visited the company's pistachio groves at Terra Bella, California. They were enthusiastically cooperative through correspondence, by telephone, and in the reading of certain first draft pages of the manuscript. At the time of final choice of essential illustrations Glen Fowler offered selections from personal files of photographs taken by him.

GRAY JOHNSON POOLE

Los Angeles, California

CONTENTS

1
ACORNS

It is a funny thing about squirrels and acorns. For most of us, the two words go together like bacon and eggs, or pork and beans.

The truth is squirrels collect, store, and eat not only acorns but all available nuts. And acorns are eaten by black bears, white-tailed deer, rats, mice, chipmunks, and raccoons; by woodpeckers, blue jays, and crows.

Long ago squirrels collected acorns under the same oak trees with Indians, pioneers, and Civil War soldiers. Squirrels today gather acorns, one by one, where farmers scoop up acorns by the ton for hog feed. *Mast* is the word for large quantities of nuts used for feeding hogs and other livestock.

There are always enough acorns to go round. Oak trees of North America annually produce more nuts than all of the region's other nut trees together, wild and cultivated. Acorns come from black oaks, so-called because of their dark gray to black bark, and from white oaks with pale gray bark.

The drawback to acorns as food for human beings is their nasty taste. Black acorns are bitter and so, too, are the acorns from most white oaks. American Indians removed the bitter

Acorns are food for wildlife.

substance from acorns by boiling and reboiling the nuts until the kernel was palatable. Acorns of a few white oak species are sweet, naturally delicious, and edible when they drop ripe from the trees.

Acorns were less important in early times than leaves of the oak tree. A medical book of ancient Greece mentions the healing of diseases with oak leaves. Pliny the Elder in his *Natural History*, first century, described a ceremony of cutting mistletoe from oak trees, sacred to Druids. The Druids, Celtic priests of Britain, Ireland, and Gaul, held their pre-Christian services in groves of oak trees, not in temples or churches. Pliny also referred to oak leaves as the material for a "civic crown" bestowed on worthy citizens of Rome.

In the United States, an oak-leaf cluster is the symbol of an additional award of a military medal. For instance, the decoration for an American wounded in battle is the Purple Heart; in recognition of a second Purple Heart, an oak-leaf cluster is pinned to the ribbon attached to the initial medal. The tiny cluster's design is made up of four oak leaves and three acorns.

"Tall oaks from little acorns grow" is a line written by David Everett in 1791. "Tall oaks" grow in the earth's temperate zone and in the highlands of Polynesia. Live oak, one white oak species found from the coast of Virginia south to eastern Texas, grows from fifty to seventy-five feet high. The best-known white oak, *Quercus alba*, state tree of Maryland, is often 100 feet tall. At maturity the low branched tree has a trunk three to four feet in diameter. Leaves of white oaks have round lobes. The lobes of black oaks are pinpointed, or bristly.

The "little acorns," round to oblong in shape, fit into cups of rough bark. Cups of some oak species are fringed around the top. When acorns are ripe the cups separate from the nuts.

Ripe acorns drop to earth in autumn. Those from black oaks

do not sprout until the following spring. White oak acorns sprout almost as soon as they hit the ground. They have to be harvested at once, before they send out shoots. The shoots sap strength from the nuts, reducing their food value. And sprouted nuts do not keep if stored by man or animal.

American Indians of forest regions depended on the crops from all nut-bearing trees, including oaks. Sweet acorns were eaten raw or roasted; bitter acorns were crushed or pulverized before being boiled to improve the taste. The paste of water and nutmeats was made into patties, or stirred, as thickening, into wild game stews. Indians used the oil from acorns as cooking grease and as a lubricant for implements.

Root-eating Indians of the West collected acorns from California white oaks and, like squirrels, stored the nuts for future use. These very sweet acorns were a staple of the Indians' winter diet. The nuts were roasted, hulled, and ground into meal, like flour. Acorn-meal loaves were baked in primitive ovens.

Settlers in America favorably compared a dish made from boiled white oak acorns with the famous boiled chestnuts of Europe. Oil skimmed from the acorn water was a popular household liniment rubbed on the body for relief of aches and pains.

Acorn remedies for various illnesses were written about in the Renaissance by Mattioli, an Italian physician. He recommended, among other acorn cures, the drinking of a mixture of milk and bitter acorn extract for treatment of snakebite and bee sting.

Union and Confederate troops of the Civil War drank an acorn substitute for coffee. Whole acorns were boiled, dry roasted, and then coarse chopped before brewing.

OPPOSITE: *White oak, state tree of Maryland.*

The bitter taste of acorns is from tannic acid, or tannin, that also is in black oak bark. The chemical compound tannin, removed from the tree bark, is important for the dyeing and tanning of leather and is an ingredient of certain kinds of ink.

Different species of oaks are lumbered for ship building; for the construction of ranch and farm fences; for the manufacture of railroad ties, furniture, wall paneling, and floors and doors.

Oaks are well-shaped shade trees planted by home-owners and included in garden designs by landscape architects.

Since oak trees are valuable in so many ways, horticulturists urge people to plant oak seedlings. Trees from the seedlings may replace oaks cut down for lumber, or may be grouped where no oaks previously grew. Eventually the trees will produce acorn crops.

Experts in the growing of nut trees look forward to the cultivation of better tasting acorns for human beings. Experiments with grafting of different species are possible. Starchy acorns may be crossed with oily acorns: small sweet acorns with larger but bitter ones.

Development of palatable new species of acorns could help to ease food shortages wherever in the world they exist.

2

WILD AND CULTIVATED

Nuts from all trees are called the fruits, and peanuts from their vines are called fruit. That can be confusing because many nuts are closely related to certain fruits; peanuts are related to some vegetables, and few trees produce true nuts.

By simple definition a nut is a dry kernel from inside a hard shell or leathery rind. That is fact as far as it goes, but there are exceptions to it as to other general statements about nuts. The so-called lychee nut, for instance, is a dried fruit with a soft center similar in texture to a raisin.

Acorns, chestnuts, and filberts, also known as hazelnuts, are true nuts, one-seeded and hard shelled. The shells of true nuts do not split open when the seed is ripe. The tough husk of a ripe coconut does not split open either, but the coconut is a fruit-related nut, a drupe.

Most nuts are drupes, a classification to which plums, peaches, cherries, and olives belong. A drupe has an outer covering, the epicarp; an inner section, the mesocarp; and, at the center, the endocarp, containing usually one seed. The seed is the nut we eat.

17

The epicarp may be as thin as plum skin. The mesocarp may contain pulp as sweet as the flesh of the peach, or be as tasteless as the soft layer of the pistachio. The endocarp may be as hard and as inedible as the olive pit, or it may be crushable like the shell of the seed of the almond tree.

In forests and on farmlands, nutting is a favorite fall activity of country children. They fill gunnysacks or pails with nuts gathered from the ground, or shinny up tree trunks to pick nuts from low limbs.

Nuts sold in city supermarkets are from cultivated trees. They are planted in groves, like fruit orchards.

Commercial growers of nuts are patient; they have to be. Nut trees grow slowly. Few species develop nuts before the trees are four years old. It takes fifteen years or more for certain kinds of trees to produce peak crops of mature nuts.

There are long waits in each stage of nut propagation, or reproduction. It takes months for seeds of some species to sprout or for seedlings to become strong. The slow processes of either grafting or budding are followed by transplantings. Years pass between seed planting and the season when growers can harvest their first crops.

Wild nuts are naturally reproduced. A nut develops under a female flower after it is fertilized by pollen from a male flower. Some species have male and female flowers on the same tree. Pollen from the male flower is either blown to a nearby female flower or, by gravity, drops onto it.

Other species have male flowers and female flowers on separate trees. Male pollen is carried to trees bearing female flowers, by wind or by insects.

A few species have *perfect* flowers, that is with both stamen, or male part, and pistil, female part. But trees with perfect flowers do not self-pollinate. More than one variety of the nut species must be planted in the orchard. Pollen from each variety pollinates the flowers of the other.

Cultivated nut trees are grown from seed—the nut kernels—and new varieties are produced by vegetative propagation. Sturdy, healthy rootstock, a rooted plant of the species, is grafted or budded with a part of a selected tree. The choice is made because of the tree's rate of growth; or the size and color of the nut, or some other good quality. The part taken from the selected tree may be a shoot with several dormant buds, or a small piece of bark with one bud. In botany, the word dormant means inactive.

Grafting and budding are done mostly in a special place, not out in the orchard. Rootstocks, in tubs or pots, are placed in an open-sided or slat-sided building. It is the grower's nursery and

Grower's nursery, showing seedling tree ready to be transplanted in the orchard.

may be roofed, or covered with a giant ceiling of canvas or synthetic fabric. A sprinkler system usually crisscrosses above the planting area.

There are several ways to graft and to bud. Whatever the method, the selected shoot, called a *scion*, is bound to the top of the rootstock with tape or with a rubber tying strip. The shoot and the rootstock grow together to form a grafted or budded tree of a new variety.

While a new tree develops it requires as much care as flowers in a greenhouse. The soil is weeded and watered. Insects are controlled. Stray shoots are clipped from the stock when the scion is set. The tape, or typing strip, is cut away a month or two after the grafting or budding.

How soon the grafted or budded trees are ready to be transplanted in the orchard depends on climate, the species of nut, and the size of the original rootstock. The grower knows from experience how to be successful with vegetative propagation. One thing he cannot do is speed up the growth of the young trees in his orchard.

The slowly maturing trees are trimmed according to their species. Stakes tied to slender trunks make them develop into straight shafts. Routine watering by irrigation or by sprays from tank trucks is required. Roots are fed by fertilizer and mulch. No matter how steady and thorough the cultivation, nuts of the new variety will not be ready to harvest for several years.

The grafting or budding of seedlings grown outdoors is called topworking. The scions grow faster on seedlings rooted in the ground instead of in pots or tubs. It still takes from three to four years to establish new varieties.

Seeds of nut trees are the kernels, or nutmeat. Ripe nuts from wild trees plop to the ground, and a certain number of the kernels naturally germinate. Sprouts become seedlings, most of which die. Only a small percentage of wild seedlings develop as full-grown trees.

Most seed nuts harvested from orchard trees have to be stratified, or prepared for germination. The ripe kernels are kept moist and cold, just above freezing, for a month and a half or two months before planting. Large seeds are selected because the size of seedlings is in proportion to the weights of the planted kernels. The treated seed, or embryo, is placed lengthwise in the ground, not up and down. The distance between planted seeds depends on when, or if, seedlings are to be transplanted. Seedlings sometimes need expert care for more than three years.

Owners of only one nut tree and growers of acres of nut trees share a problem: wildlife pests. It is not easy to get rid of them whether they are large or small, four-footed or feathered. Many kinds of defense are tried.

Squirrels and birds, in that order, are the most destructive predators of nuts in all stages of development. Blasts from a shotgun will successfully shoo flocks of birds, or will temporarily scare off a couple of neighborhood crows. Other noisemakers serve the same purpose, but their effects are not permanent, either.

One homemade device is constructed of a tin can containing a handful of marbles. A string from the can is attached to an electric motor connected to a timer. The timer goes off. The motor starts. The string jerks. The can jiggles. The marbles roll and make a great rattle inside the tin. A series of cans attached to the same motor create a racket loud enough to scatter birds.

Ornithologists have recorded the alarm calls of birds. Broadcasts of the distress or warning signals frighten birds on the wing or in trees. But it costs a great deal of money to install orchard loudspeakers wired to a phonograph turntable in a shed somewhere on the grounds.

The owner of one nut tree can keep squirrels away from ripening nuts with metal. A wide band around the trunk prevents squirrels from getting a foothold on the slippery surface. The band has to be loose enough to give the tree trunk room to expand as it grows.

There is a catch to the metal band device. It works only for a tree standing alone. If other kinds of trees are closeby, squirrels can leap from them to the limbs of the nut-bearing tree.

Shooting is the most common way to get rid of squirrels in a commercial nut orchard. There is a catch to that system, too. If the orchard is planted close to a forest, reserve squirrels, like troops in battle, move out of the woods to replace the squirrels killed.

Mice are destructive in a grower's nursery and to young trees in the orchard. Mice eat seeds, the roots of seedlings, and tender bark. Poison and traps for the little rodents are placed inside the nursery. Or a protective screen of galvanized mesh hardware cloth is installed around the outside. The mesh cloth is sunk from six to twelve inches into the earth to keep field mice from tunneling into the nursery area.

Tar paper wrapped around young orchard trees repels both mice and rabbits. Trunk shields are sometimes made of the galvanized mesh hardware cloth. Like the metal band protector against squirrels, the mesh cloth shield must be loose to permit expansion of the growing trunk.

Removal of weeds and grass around each individual seedling in an orchard is another expensive way to protect young growth from mice. Mice have no place to nest, feed, or hide if the ground around seedlings is bare. Even mulch for fertilizing the soil is often raked from around seedlings when they are dormant, or not in a growing period of the year.

There are manufactured repellents for spraying on nut trees

and their seeds. The repellents, unpleasant to taste or smell or touch, are practical only when a few pests are present.

Rabbits, but not deer, stay away from seedlings sprayed with repellents. It is very difficult to protect the juicy leaves of seedlings from hungry deer. In a region where deer are numerous, wire fencing may be staked around nut groves and nurseries.

Conservationists recognize the importance of planting and protecting wild nut trees. In the first half of the twentieth century, reckless lumbering reduced the number of nut-bearing trees. Mammals and birds, deprived of a major food source, either died off or failed to breed. Wildlife population decreased.

Improved timber management is slowly restoring the balance of available wild nuts and of the wildlife dependent on them for food.

Replacement of nut trees in forest and woodlands close to orchards helps to keep wildlife away from the cultivated trees. For the same purpose, trees with nuts enjoyed by animals are planted around commercial groves. By providing nut trees specifically for wildlife, growers are able to harvest more nuts from their own orchards.

Harvested by the millions of pounds a year, nuts for commercial use are run through processing plants. Sorted and washed nuts in their shells are sold in bulk. Shelled nuts, packaged in tin, glass, or bags, may be plain, dry roasted, salted, or otherwise seasoned. Crushed nuts produce oil for cooking and for salad dressings, for medicines and cosmetics.

By-products of nut processing provide materials for many manufactured objects as you will find out in various chapters of this book.

Leftovers from harvesting and processing are called trash, and even trash is not wasted. One of its important uses is as feed for livestock and poultry.

3
BRAZIL NUT

In groups of up to twenty-four, Brazil nuts fill the seed pod of a large fruit. The fruit grows on trees found in remote northern areas of the South American country for which it is named. Efforts to cultivate Brazil nut trees fail everywhere, even in Brazil. Some few experimental trees are planted there in orchards, called plantations.

Nearly 100 percent of Brazil nuts come from wild trees. They are in dense forests stretching along the banks of the Amazon River and its tributaries, some not much larger than creeks.

Brazil nut trees are evergreen and huge. Their straight trunks reach heights of 100 to 150 feet and branch high above the ground. The diameter of the base of an old tree may be as much as six feet. Wide leaves, bright green and textured like leather, are twelve to fifteen inches long. Large cream-colored flowers of the trees have six big petals.

Fruit of the Brazil nut tree ripens from November to June. It is dark brown, shaped a little like a pear, and normally measures from four to six inches in diameter. At maturity, the fruit usually weighs two to four pounds. The diameter can sometimes be eight inches, and the weight fifteen pounds.

The fruit's half-inch thick outer crust, or skin, is brittle. Woody pulp surrounds an inner, very hard pod containing twelve to twenty-four seeds—the Brazil nuts. The dark brown shells, up to two inches long, are triangular in shape. They fit, side by side, into the outer pod like stick candy hand-packed into a glass jar.

If you have ever used a nutcracker on a Brazil nut, you know how much strength it takes to break the shell. It is cracked more easily by a hammer, but the blow may shatter and damage the kernel.

When seeds are ripe, the fruit drops from the trees. Various animals, including monkeys, try to force open a trapdoor at the base of the seed pod. A greedy monkey, reaching in for a seed, will not release the nut even if caught in the opening. That is why Brazil nuts are often called monkeypots.

Certain South American trees of the same genus *Lecythis* are called monkeypot trees. Some actually have seed pods large enough for small monkeys to live in.

Brazil nuts are gathered by natives of the region or by migrant workers. The harvesters are occasionally knocked out when hit on the head by falling fruit.

The nut crop is taken from the forest by small boats to nearby villages. From there, dealers ship the nuts on the river to harbor cities. A quarter of the crop is shelled before export, chiefly from the city of Pará. Pará nut is another name for the Brazil nut.

The nut trees are important to the economy of Brazil. Ships are locally caulked with the bark. Oil extracted from the rich nuts is burned in lamps to light rural huts and serves as a home remedy ointment. Commercially, the oil is an ingredient of perfume, soap, lacquer, and varnish.

In countries of export, Brazil nuts are sold in the shell, by bulk; in salted nut mixtures; or for making candies and baked goods.

The sweet, flavorful nuts, high in protein and oil content, are not part of the staple Brazilian diet. The climate is too hot for people to eat substantial amounts of so oily a food. When working hard and in need of quick nourishment, road-building crews along the Amazon or men gathering the nut crop may eat a few of the Brazil nuts in the course of a day.

For the most part, Brazil nuts are enjoyed as a delicacy in foreign lands thousands of miles from where they grow.

4

LYCHEE

The lychee nut is a small fruit called a nut, when dried.

According to legend lychees caused a war in ancient China. As the story goes, a beautiful girl in an emperor's court liked fresh and dried lychees better than any food. Eager to please his lovely subject, the emperor sent soldiers to a distant province where lychees grew. The troops, under orders to uproot lychee trees, after harvesting their fruit, battled to victory. Whether captured lychee trees taken back to the emperor stayed alive and healthy in his realm will never be known.

Lychees cannot be made to flourish unless the weather is exactly right. They will not grow in the tropics which have year-round heat and high humidity. Flowers and fruit develop in a drought but not in an unseasonable, rainy year. The ideal conditions are subtropical: long hot spells, short cold snaps, and some rainfall.

Lychees were not identified away from their native China until 1775. That year trees were recognized on the island of Jamaica in the British West Indies. Today lychees are cultivated in certain Mediterranean areas and in parts of India, South America, Hawaii, and the United States mainland. The

Typically beautiful lychee tree.

first American crop ripened in Florida in 1916. By the mid-twentieth century there were a few lychee trees in California.

A lychee tree is beautiful. Its warty-looking ripe fruit is not. The trees, only thirty to forty feet tall, curve down like an open umbrella. Tips of the branches almost touch the ground. Orchard trees are planted twenty-five to thirty-five feet apart to allow space for the spread of the wide canopy of foliage.

The leaves are reddish when first sprouted but turn bright green and remain that color for the life of the tree. Feathery greenish flowers stick up from the leaf bunches.

The fruit, which is about the size of a strawberry, has a thin, papery outer cover with small round bumps. The skin, yellow to red in color, surrounds juicy, whitish pulp. At the center is a dark brown seed, relatively large and hard.

The fresh fruit is very sweet. Some say its flavor resembles that of the Muscat grape from which wine is made. Like lychees,

The warty-looking lychee fruit is a nut when dried.

Muscats are often dried, and then taste sugary. Lychee fruit is eaten raw, put up in cans, and made into preserves. It is best known as the lychee nut. After it is dried, the lychee is firm, sweet, very dark in color, and seems like a nut with a raisinlike center.

Pomologists, horticulturists who work with fruits, are experimenting with lychees. The pomologists hope to develop lychee varieties for a wider range of climate conditions and to improve lychee fruit bearing. Even cultivated trees bear good crops only once in every three or four years.

Lychees are propagated by air-layering, a system used for plants impossible to cultivate by grafting and budding. Two kinds of air-layering are suitable for lychees. A shoot or a branch of a parent plant is bent to the ground for rooting. While rooting the shoot is kept covered with wet soil or damp moss.

When a pot, or box, tops the moist material, the method is called pot-layering. The use of heavy string to keep the wet soil or damp moss in place is known as Chinese-layering.

A rooted shoot, or branch, ready for planting, is cut away from the parent stock. An air-layered tree begins to bear fruit in three to five years.

The most confusing thing about the lychee is its name. Most horticulturists call it lychee. Dictionaries usually list it as *litchi*. Menus in Chinese restaurants where preserved and dried lychees are served may give other spellings.

You might like to play a game with the name. Keep a list of spelling variations as you see them in dictionaries, encyclopedias, and other books; on labels of cans and jars; in market advertisements; on menus. Your first four listings undoubtedly will be lychee, litchi, leechee, lichee. And then what?

5

PISTACHIO

Smiling nuts please growers of pistachio trees. When pistachios are ripe each shell opens to a shape resembling the curved up, happy grin on a human face. If bad weather or disease or pests prevent pistachios from ripening, the shells do not split open. Growers then sadly repeat an old Turkish expression, "Too bad, our pistachios are not smiling."

Pistachios smile when ripe.

Pistachio trees may have originated in Central Asia. No one knows the exact location, or the time in history. The nuts supposedly were taken to India, and afterward to the Middle East where they thrive.

The pistachio nut, seed of the tree, is greenish in color, oblong in shape, and three-quarters of an inch to one inch in length.

Although wild trees were few in number in ancient times, the nuts were well known and highly prized. Popularity of pistachios increased with cultivation through many centuries, but the supply has never matched the demand. There has been a lack of balance between available nuts and eager customers, because pistachio trees will grow and produce crops only in certain climates.

The Queen of Sheba, while reigning in Assyria, took the entire crop from the limited number of pistachio trees in that country. Only she and her honored guests enjoyed the nuts as food. By decree of the queen, no subject outside the royal household was allowed to keep any part of the pistachio harvest.

The Roman Emperor Vitellius, A.D. 69, planted pistachios in Italy, and one of his generals carried seed nuts to Spain. The rare nuts were treats served at family celebrations and on holidays, a custom continuing today in Europe and in the Middle East.

A Syrian immigrant introduced pistachios into the United States in the late 1890s. Before migrating to America, he was a nut salesman in Syria and Turkey, traveling his territory by camel. He first imported pistachios for his family and friends in New York. In 1906 he became a dealer, and other East Coast competitors soon followed his lead.

They imported pistachios from Turkey, Iran, Afghanistan, Syria, and Italy. Fewer nuts for export were grown in Greece, India, Tunisia, Pakistan, and Lebanon.

32

At first pistachios were already roasted and salted when shipped to the United States. The original importer became an American processor of raw nuts in 1917.

Nutmeats were bought by candy manufacturers, by ice cream makers, and by bakers, for flavoring batter and cake icing. Pistachios in the shell were variously treated for retail sale. Some were dyed red to conceal mottled markings caused by natural drying of the nuts. Other shells were whitened with heavy coats of salt and cornstarch. Unblemished shells, few in number, were simply roasted and salted.

At the turn of the twentieth century, a few pistachio trees were planted in a part of California with suitable climate. On the East Coast the business of processing and marketing imported pistachios continued. Experiments with the cultivation of pistachio trees steadily increased in the Sacramento and San Joaquin Valleys, collectively known as the Central Valley of California.

Pistachios do well where summers are long and hot; winters, short and cold. These are the normal weather conditions in the Central Valley.

Wild pistachios exist in desert regions of the Middle East where there is no other tree, no bush, no flower, and hardly a sprig of grass. Trees leaf and their nuts develop better under drought conditions than where there is high humidity, too much dampness.

For the best results cultivated trees need soil moisture. When necessary, regular watering is applied from early spring until the start of the harvest in late August. But, like some ornamental shrubs and certain flowers in pots, pistachio trees should never have "wet feet." Nurserymen use the expression "wet feet" to describe standing water around the base of a tree or plant.

Pistachio trees, fifteen to twenty feet tall, are typically shaped like apple trees. Flowers, greenish-brown, are neither showy nor attractive. The nuts are in clusters, like bunches of grapes.

A plant explorer, Dr. W.E. Whitehouse, collected pistachio seed nuts when in Iran and Turkestan for several months of 1929. His work was done for a program of the United States Department of Agriculture (USDA).

Many seedlings from the Whitehouse collection were grown at Chico, north of Sacramento, state capital of California. Research was directed by Lloyd E. Joley, horticulturist, at the Plant Introduction Station, USDA. He planned and supervised experiments with cultivation, orchard procedures, and the processing of harvested nuts.

Increased production of marketable pistachios is the purpose of continuing research at Chico and at other USDA stations. Experiments are also done by agriculture departments of several American colleges and by commercial growers.

Experts do not plant pistachios where cotton, tomatoes, or melons previously grew. Diseases of those plants, if still in the earth, reduce the yield of pistachio trees.

Before planting, soil is tested to find out what fertilizer should be used, which nutrients added. Pistachios require few nutrients, but the earth has to be harrowed and dug to give good drainage.

In foreign countries from which pistachios are exported to the United States, alternate bearing is a problem. Trees have good crops one year, poor the next. Experiments to assure uniform annual crops began in the California valleys.

W.D. Fowler was a pioneer in the cultivation of pistachio trees in the San Joaquin Valley. Before 1954 citrus fruits were the main crops of his farm management business at Terra Bella, California. That year he set out seventy-seven pistachio trees, as a test project.

More trees were planted at Terra Bella and at Madera, 100 miles to the north. Fowler traveled from orchard to orchard by plane. He inspected the trees from the air and, close at hand, on the ground. A chemical engineer by profession, he experimented with propagation of pistachios and invented machinery for processing.

Representatives of the company traveled to the Middle East to find suitable rootstock varieties of pistachios for cultivation. Seed nuts from the Greek island of Chios were chosen for planting.

Following Fowler's death in 1971, his company went forward with plans for expansion. Planted acres totaled 4000 by 1973, when the Terra Bella nursery contained nearly 350,000 seedlings. Improvement of orchard and processing plant methods continued.

Seedlings and budded stock remain in the nursery from one year to a year and a half. Propagation is done to insure high yield, or the most possible number of ripe nuts per tree, and the production of larger nuts.

The Fowlers and other commercial growers favored the Kerman variety for purposes of propagation. Over a twelve to fifteen year period, the Kerman doubled the number of nuts per acre per tree of the next highest producing variety.

Pistachios have male and female flowers on separate trees. The Kerman is a female tree. One well-known male variety is called Peters. It was named for the man who discovered it near Fresno in the early 1900s. Trees of the variety probably were transported from the Middle East by Armenians who, in large numbers, had migrated to Fresno.

Male and female trees are set out in the grove in a ratio of one male to five to ten females. Ideally, the blooming time for both sexes coincides so male pollen is ready when female flowers

Unripe pistachios on tree.

open. Since insects do not pollinate pistachios, machine blowers sometimes are used to help the wind spread pollen.

Pistachio trees are not ready to bear fruit until six or seven years after budding. Trees mature no earlier than fifteen years of age, no later than twenty but bear peak crops until at least age fifty. An acre of healthy trees gives a yearly crop of more than 4000 pounds of pistachio nuts.

Foreign methods of pistachio harvest are primitive. Women do most of the work in the groves, spreading pistachios out in the sun to dry. The natural drying process is slow and causes the uneven mottling seen on many shells of imported pistachios.

Harvest by hand labor is impractical for American commercial crops. In 1961 W.D. Fowler adapted machinery used for the harvest of other kinds of nuts and invented equipment specifically for his pistachio processing plant.

One machine shakes trees when the pistachios are ready for harvest. Clusters fall onto a conveyor belt and are emptied into containers. The nuts are kept off the ground to prevent dirt from getting into the split shells. With the shaker and conveyor, two men can harvest an acre of nuts in one hour.

At the processing plant, pistachios with non-split shells are mechanically separated from split nuts. An electric-eye sorting machine processes 2000 pounds of nuts an hour. Ninety percent of the ripe nuts are the same size, but they are shaken to insure uniformity; the very few too-small nuts are removed. Butane dryers rapidly dehydrate the nuts. A special machine for pistachios roasts the nuts plain, or flavored with salt.

The epicarp of pistachios is nutritious as cattle feed. The inner shell from non-split nuts is ground into a filler for cattle feed. The endocarp also is used in the manufacture of a cleaner for automobile paint.

Edible pistachios have their greatest popularity in the United

States where ninety-eight percent of the world supply is consumed. Experts estimate that by the mid-1980s American consumption of edible pistachios could be more than 60 million pounds at a market value of well over $100 million.

Export countries send what they can, when they can. The amount is not predictable from year to year, because alternate bearing remains a problem with foreign crops.

The number of nuts projected for worldwide consumption is much more than original research experimenters and commercial growers even optimistically expected. The increase of pistachios, now in short supply, has to come from American groves.

Orchards, now maturing in the United States, may provide the bulk of tomorrow's smiling pistachios.

6

ALMOND

In Biblical times almonds were even more important than pistachios. There are more then seventy references to almonds or almond wood in the Old Testament.

How the rod of Aaron, brother of Moses, was turned into an almond branch is described in Numbers, chapter 17, verse 8. The rod "put forth buds, and produced blossoms, and bare ripe almonds."

The budding of another rod of almond wood is one of many legends about Tannhäuser, a German *minnesinger* who lived in the thirteenth century. *Minnesingers* were poets who either sang their verses, or recited them to musical accompaniment.

Tannhäuser, the poet and musician, was in disgrace with the Pope of his time. Face to face with Tannhäuser, the angry Pope held high his staff and shook it. He said there was no more chance for Tannhäuser to be forgiven his sins than for the staff, or rod, of almond wood to blossom.

After Tannhäuser went far away, the papal staff did burst into almond buds. The Pope sent messengers to offer forgiveness to the *minnesinger* who died without receiving the word. Tannhäuser's name is now famous because of the opera written about him by Richard Wagner in the mid-nineteenth century.

In the Tuscany region of Italy, forked sticks of almond wood were long ago supposed to be treasure finders. When a stick, held in the hand, turned itself down toward the ground, people dug deep. They hoped to find buried gold or jewels beneath the spot where the stick pointed. The forked sticks of Tuscany were like divining rods, or dowsers, for locating underground water or minerals.

Shelled almonds and raisins, combined, were early symbols of good luck for Jews. The nuts and fruits, packaged together, are still popular in Eastern Europe. An old Yiddish lullaby called "Raisins and Almonds" is today a song well known in Jewish families.

In Greece almonds are offered for good fortune at christenings, weddings, and the ordinations of priests. The nuts, in uneven numbers, three, five, seven, are given to guests at the celebrations. Even at simple weddings of the humblest Greeks, the traditional almonds are offered.

The custom of giving good-luck almonds to wedding guests is followed in other countries. The nuts are wrapped in white tulle, tied with satin ribbon or, for fancy receptions, placed in tiny baskets or doll-sized slippers. These are decorated with white net, often with gold-colored wedding rings sewn to it.

The favors are always Jordan almonds. Those almonds are mostly sold with shiny sugar coating. The candy part may be white, as for wedding receptions, or pastel or bright colored. Jordan almonds are from Malaga in Spain. The word "Jordan" is from the French *jardin*, meaning garden.

Almonds originated in southwest Asia. They are commercially grown chiefly in Spain, Portugal, Morocco, Italy, and in California. The cultivated almond orchards there are located in the Sacramento and San Joaquin valleys.

Spanish missionaries probably introduced the almond into California during the eighteenth century. Experiments with new varieties began, on a small scale, about the middle of the nineteenth century. In January, 1897, seventy-one almond growers formed a cooperative organization for processing and marketing their nuts. The co-op steadily increased its membership and became the California Almond Growers Exchange (CAGE) with headquarters in Sacramento.

In its first year the growers' association sold twenty-five tons of almonds; fifty-eight years later, in 1955, their tonnage was 25,000. By 1970 the total production of California almonds by both CAGE members and other growers was well over 135 million pounds of nuts. More than 210,000 acres of almond groves included 75,000 acres of young trees, not then full bearing.

Those statistics represent hard work by hundreds of industrious men and thousands of busy bees.

Almond trees lose their leaves in autumn. In late February

Almonds with leaves on tree branches.

PRUNUS AMYGDALUS KAPAREIL

and early March, beautiful pink blossoms cover the tree limbs before new leaves develop. The almond flower is one of the perfect type with pistil and stamen. But like most other trees with perfect flowers, almonds do not satisfactorily self-pollinate. Their heavy, sticky pollen is carried by insects.

In California orchards the insect is the honeybee. Beehives are set out in the groves in groups of ten to fifteen, allowing one colony up to three colonies for each acre of trees.

Almond orchards require year-round care. Soil is fertilized and treated with nutrients. The earth must be moist from blossoming through the dry, hot growing season. Orchards are irrigated, even occasionally flooded, under controlled conditions. But too much rain at the wrong times of year is bad.

Rainy weather in spring cuts down the activity of bees and reduces their transfer of pollen. Rainy weather in summer holds back nut development and may cause diseases.

The trees are delicate. They are injured by many insects, including those with such strange names as fruit-tree leaf roller, the codling moth, and the Pacific flat-headed borer. Among numerous attacking diseases are hull rot, leafscab, shot-hole fungus, and the viruses: ring spot, almond mosaic, and almond calico.

Weird-looking machinery and devices are seen in the orchards. Those for protecting the trees are huge sprayers, portable heaters, and stationary wind machines.

The sprayers have dozens of nozzles, like so many halos, around wheels big as those of a trailer truck. Once in midwinter and again in late spring, sprayers move through the rows of trees and shoot out insect repellents.

Heaters in the orchards combat spring frosts that shrivel blossoms and hurt young nuts. The heaters, similar to small stoves, come in various styles, all designed for antipollution operation.

Wind machines warm almond orchards.

Heaters may brighten an orchard six or eight times in a season or, in other years, only on a couple of nippy nights. The number of heaters varies with the location of the orchard. There may be as many as one to every other tree in every other row of trees.

Wind machines can also warm some orchards. A blower is

installed on a platform at the top of a permanently placed column, higher than the twenty- to thirty-foot trees. The blower of the tower machine can produce 17 million BTUs (British thermal units) of warm air per hour. But the system works only when air forty feet up is warmer than the air at ground level.

Two giant machines, the hydraulic knocker and a plowlike sweeper, roll through the orchards at harvest time. Hulls of ripe almonds split open and begin to dry. The shell, the kernel, and its skin also dry. When an entire crop is ready, knockers rumble through the orchard, violently shaking trees until the ground vibrates. Nuts drop like enormous hailstones.

A few days later, sweepers scoop up tons of nuts. Hulls are removed and processed for cattle feed. The nuts start through a plant where they are prepared for marketing, chiefly as food for people.

Marzipan is the most famous almond sweet. Made chiefly from finely ground almonds and sugar, it is spread between cake layers, made into macaroons, or formed into miniature candies in fruit and vegetable shapes.

Almonds—slivered, diced, sliced—are ingredients in many recipes for dessert and main course dishes. Flour made from ground almonds with most of the oil removed is sometimes prescribed for the diet of people suffering with diabetes.

Almond oil is the base for the food flavoring, almond extract. The oil is an ingredient of face creams, hand lotions, and other cosmetics, as well as of certain medicines. Almonds rubbed on the skin or taken internally were recommended as sunburn treatment nearly twenty centuries ago.

The almond in commerce is today a source of food, manufactured by-products, and income to growers and processors. It undoubtedly will continue to be a worldwide symbol of good luck.

7

MACADAMIA

What would you answer if someone asked you to have another kindal-kindal? That hyphenated word is one of at least a dozen names for the macadamia nut, native to Australia. The nuts originally grew wild in the Australian states of Queensland and New South Wales. Among other regional names for the macadamia are bauple nut, nut oak, maroochy, Australian nut, Queensland nut, and gympie nut, for the seaport Gympie in Queensland.

Kindal-kindal was the word of aborigines who ate the nuts for hundreds of years before outsiders settled the continent. The popularity of the nut there is credited to Dr. John Macadam (1827–1865), a scientist from Scotland. While living in Australia he talked enthusiastically about the fine flavor of the nut subsequently named for him.

There are more varieties of macadamias than nicknames. Trees vary in height, in spread of top leaves, and in color of blossoms, ranging from white to cream to pink, the most beautiful.

The half-inch long flowers cluster on hanging stalks. Stalks may be as short as two inches, or as long as a foot and a half,

Macadamia nuts in shell.

there may be as few as fifty sweet-scented flowers, or as many as 300. The leaves, like those of holly, are evergreen and notched; some are prickly. Seedling trees produce full crops in three to seven years; mature trees produce full crops at twelve to fifteen years.

Cultivated macadamias were first planted in Australia about 1870. The native nut does well in all of the subtropical areas of the country, but orchards are planted, where possible, in volcanic soil.

Macadamia trees for garden shade and as curiosities were introduced into the Hawaiian Islands in 1878 and into California in 1879. Hawaii was the ideal location for macadamias. The soil is all volcanic, a mixture of rich earth and lava from volcano eruptions. Weather throughout the chain of islands is suitable for macadamia cultivation.

Rainfall in Hawaii is from 150 to 200 inches a year, or four to five times as much as the minimum needed by macadamias. Rainfall in eastern Australia is sixty to ninety inches and, in the region of California where macadamias are planted, only twelve inches. Californian cultivated macadamia groves are irrigated.

Statistics about Hawaiian production of macadamias are in big figures. The first commercial orchard was established on a few acres in 1916. By 1971 and 1972 more than 14 million pounds of nuts were annually produced in Hawaii.

The crops came from 9250 acres of trees, many not full bearing. On the basis of the expected mature trees, the State Department of Agriculture of Hawaii in 1973 predicted the production of 45 million pounds of nuts per year by 1980.

Macadamias are the third largest crop of Hawaii; pineapples and sugar cane are the leaders. The island of Hawaii, known as the Big Island, provides ninety-nine percent of the Hawaiian macadamias and ninety-five percent of the world supply.

In Hawaii macadamia trees commonly grow to about forty feet and have an upper spread of leaves of the same measurement. Some macadamia species are sixty feet tall with a leaf crown of fifty feet or more. The proportion of height to width is excellent for a shade tree or an ornamental; that is the horticultural word for a plant or tree grown purely for decoration.

Macadamia roots are very shallow, and the trees are easily blown over by a strong gust. Orchard sites should be in locations free from high winds. Rows of Norfolk pines are planted as windbreaks around Hawaiian groves.

Flowers contain both pistils and stamens and, under certain conditions, trees self-pollinate. Honeybees, again, as with al-

Macadamia grove in the Hawaiian Islands.

monds, are the chief pollinators.

The trees are not true everbearing types, although they put forth a few blossoms and produce some ripe nuts all through the year. Major Hawaiian crops are concentrated over a period of seven months, from late spring into November. Growers everywhere are trying to propagate macadamias with shorter crop seasons, to reduce the cost of harvest.

The crunchy sweet, white macadamia kernel is round. So is its hard brown shell, covered with an outer husk. When the nuts are ripe, they drop from the trees. Since there is no way to find out how much of a crop is ripe on the trees, owners must wait to be shown by the falling nuts.

Mechanical harvesters scoop up nuts from level ground. Where ground is uneven, harvest is by hand, a slow and costly method.

One commercial grower devised a clever trap for catching ripe nuts from trees growing on 175 bumpy acres. The orchard was planted on a total of 1200 acres of lava land near Hilo. Jungle growth was cleared away, leaving 1025 acres of level ground.

When trees on the uneven ground matured, heavy netting was attached under their branches. Ripe nuts, like children on a playground slide, rolled down the net and dropped into collection bins. The ingenious invention for harvesting is now patented.

Outer husks are stripped off by machines in processing plants. The nuts are then dehydrated to remove almost every bit of moisture before being separated by size.

Shells are cracked by steel rollers. When processing began in Hawaii, macadamias had the hardest shells of any nut. The cracking machine had to be strong yet designed to keep the round kernel whole. Development of thinner shells is one research project of botanists.

Most shelled kernels are roasted in coconut oil and dunked in salt powder. Some few unsalted nuts are sold in Honolulu for the manufacture of candy, ice cream, and baked goods. Nearly all exported macadamias are salted. They are packed in jars, cans, bags for food stores, and snack packets for airline meal trays.

There have been small groves of macadamias in Florida since the 1920s and specimen trees in California since the last of the nineteenth century. But orchards in California were not planted until after the return of World War II servicemen. They learned to enjoy macadamia nuts while stationed in or shipping through the Hawaiian Islands.

Research and experiments with propagation of macadamias is done in several Australian and Californian centers, at the University of Hawaii, in Florida, Costa Rica, and at Kingston, Jamaica, in the British West Indies.

Macadamia trees are very free from diseases and from damage by insects and animals. Outside of Australia, no part of the tree, not even the nut, is eaten by wildlife.

Whether the macadamia will become a major food for people is a question to be answered in the next quarter of a century. By then, thousands of trees will have reached maturity.

8

WALNUTS

"Add to the cookie batter one-half cup of Persian walnuts" is a recipe instruction few American cooks would understand.

The Persian walnut is known as the English walnut and, increasingly, as the California walnut. The long-famous nut originated in ancient Persia (now Iran). For hundreds of years Persians shipped the nuts east to the Orient and west to Europe. After England became a powerful trading nation in the mid-fourteenth century, Persian nuts were mostly cargo in the vessels of British owners. That is how the term English walnut came to common usage.

The walnut part of the name for the nut is even more complicated. Dictionaries give an English origin through a word with various spellings, often *wahlnut*, loosely meaning foreign nut.

Persian walnuts do grow in England, but weather there is never hot enough for the production of bountiful crops. On the East Coast of the United States, trees of a hardy type of Persians were planted by German immigrants. Spanish missionaries probably took the walnut into California in the eighteenth century. A commercial orchard of 200 trees was planted in 1869 with walnut varieties shipped from Chile, but of French origin.

Walnuts flourished wherever they were planted in California. Summers are dry and hot enough for fruit development; winters have just enough cold days for a necessary dormant period.

In a century the walnut industry of California increased from 200 trees to 164,000 acres of trees. A growers' cooperative, founded in 1912, is now Diamond Walnut Growers, Inc., with headquarters at Stockton and a membership of 5000.

Most southern California orchards have been plowed under for various reasons: cost of irrigation, high taxes, lack of labor for the orchards, and rising land values.

Northern orchards, chiefly in the Central Valley, produce ninety-five percent of the American commercial crop of Persian walnuts. There are some commercial orchards in Oregon and a very few in the state of Washington.

Persian walnut trees and black walnut trees, belonging to the same group, or genus, are valued for their wood. The black walnut, native to North America, has been of major importance in cabinetmaking since Colonial days. Both of the two walnut trees are lumbered for furniture. Their wood is prized by sculptors, planed for veneer and paneling, made into decorative boxes and other objects, and used for gunstocks and musical instruments.

The black walnut is a wild forest tree throughout a wide area of the eastern United States. It is also planted in farm country as an ornamental, for shade, and for the nut crop as food for people and wildlife.

There are plantations of black walnuts being grown for timber of the future. Trees cultivated for lumber need constant care and orchard techniques are complex. Annual nut crops bring the grower some return for his time, work, and expense of

Persian walnuts with husks open.

upkccp, but his investment does not pay off for thirty to forty years. That is when the logs are ready for lumbering.

Since 1915 research botanists have experimented with the black walnut, trying to improve quality, to reduce the shell thickness, and to increase the size of the crop—the number of harvested nuts. In spite of advances in methods of cultivation, most processed black walnuts are from wild trees.

Walnuts are large trees. The Persians grow forty to sixty feet, with leaf spread to match. The black walnuts are often 100 feet high and have trunks nearly three feet in diameter. The trunk of a tree grown for timber may be ten to twelve feet in diameter. Both Persian and black walnuts produce nuts for a long time; some when more than 100 years old and even, it is said, at 200 years, or more.

The two walnuts are self-fertile, with male and female flowers on the same tree. In California groves where uniform production of crops is essential, pollinization can be a problem. The female flowers may blossom before the male flowers develop their pollen. Or male pollen may be ready before the female flowers open.

An elaborate pattern of tree planting takes advantage of prevailing winds for spreading pollen for cross-pollinization. For example, a variety with male flowers known to produce pollen at a certain time is planted upwind from trees of a variety with female flowers of the same blossoming date.

Scheduled planting is not the only means of helping nature. Another method is to store pollen until female flowers are open. The pollen is then put into small open mesh bags, each containing a heavy stone. The six-inch square bag, on a long cord, is tossed to the top of a tree with open female blossoms. The stone weight holds the mesh bag in place; the cord is fastened to the base of the tree.

Pollen in the bag is shaken out either by a hard yank on the anchored string or a tap from the end of a long pole. To be sure

Walnut harvester in groves.

of pollinization fresh bags of pollen, like hooks on fishing lines, are cast to the treetop over a period of several days.

Harvest in California is from mid-September until December 1. Trees have their first marketable crops at age six and are mature and full bearing at twelve.

During harvest, shakers on wheels go through the orchards three to four times, loosening only ripe nuts. The nuts are picked up from the ground by hand or mechanically.

The most sophisticated mechanical picker is a large machine with many attachments and moving parts. It picks up the nuts, throws off orchard trash and leaves, send the nuts up an inclined shoot and over to an attached trailer. On the way to the processing plants, any remaining green outer husks are removed, and the shells are washed, right on the trailer.

At the processing plant the walnuts are fumigated, bleached for uniform appearance of the shells, culled twice, dried, and sorted by size. Some are marketed in-shell; more are shelled before being packed in glass or tin, or packaged in see-through bags.

Most Persian walnuts used to be sold in-shell, because the shells are so easy to crack with the touch of a hammer, or with any kind of nutcracker. Even so, the popularity of shelled walnuts increased and, by 1970, more than sixty percent were shelled before marketing.

Black walnuts have very hard shells and, for the most part, are sold in kernels, out of the shell. The rough shell is brown, much darker than the smooth, light tan shell of the Persian walnut.

The black walnut kernel is in two parts, like the Persian, but does not fill its shell. The Persian kernel, two-sided in perfectly matched shapes, fills its shell; the shell also has matched sides, closed tight along a lengthwise rib.

Persian walnuts have easy-to-crack shells.

Neither the black nor the Persian walnut is roasted. The Persians are primarily for munching. They are included in most assortments of in-shell nuts and, at holiday times, are served in-shell with dried Muscats. The attractive half kernels of shelled Persian walnuts decorate various kinds of sweets.

The black walnut is less popular for nibbling, because the kernel's flavor, by itself, is too strong for enjoyment by most people. But the flavor is prized when the nuts are combined with other ingredients for baking, in batter and icing, and for the manufacture of both candies and ice cream.

Black walnuts are valuable diet supplements because of their high protein content and low sugar and starch content.

In early times Persian walnuts were used as medication. An ancient Roman suggested chewed walnuts mixed with saliva as salve for treatment of the bite of a mad dog. The nuts were once said to prevent tooth decay and, long after, juice from the tree root was applied to gums to relieve toothache. An extract of Persian walnuts was given to patients with tuberculosis.

Persian walnut oil was one of several kinds experimented with by the Van Eyck brothers, Hubert and Jan, Flemish painters born in the fourteenth century. They were the first artists to mix oil with paints. Walnut oil was also added to paints by the Italian artist Correggio (1494–1534).

A by-product of walnut processing today is its fast-drying oil for paint used in industry. That by-product is only one of dozens listed in *The California Nut*, a publication of the Diamond Walnut Growers.

After oil is extracted from the residue of walnut processing, a cake remains. The cake is reduced to meal which is sold as food for poultry and for commercially grown worms.

Various forms of processed shells go into snow tires, insecticides, blasting powder, asphalt roofing, firebrick, hard flooring, hard rubber products, battery boxtops, and oil drilling equipment.

Shells of black walnuts fertilize tobacco fields and blue grass pastures; the hulls are added to compost piles.

A shell material, coarse ground, is used for sandblasting and the cleaning and polishing of metals: a very fine grind, like flour, in the manufacturing of plastics and glue, and a medium grind, about like table salt, for fur cleaning.

Brown wool dye is made from the leaves, bark, and hulls of Persian walnuts, black walnuts, and from another of their genus —the butternut.

Uniforms of many Confederate soldiers in the Civil War

were colored with brown dye distilled from unripe butternuts. Because of the "butternut jeans" worn by the soldiers, they and their sympathizers were nicknamed butternuts. Confederate troops, in the mountains of West Virginia, Tennessee, and Kentucky, doctored themselves with numerous remedies made from the bark and roots of butternut trees.

Earlier in American history, Indians applied butternut bark as a cure for rheumatism, headache, and toothache. They treated fresh wounds with a strong solution of boiled butternut bark.

In some future time black and Persian walnuts could be even more useful than today. They might provide cooking oil for American kitchens. The oil now is naturally unstable, subject to change and deterioration. But a process may one day be developed for the production of walnut cooking oil.

9

PECAN

Spanish and French settlers mistook the native American pecan for a walnut. One Frenchman in Mississippi, wrote, in the early eighteenth century, "The Natives have three kinds of walnut trees. . . ." He liked best the smallest nuts that ". . . are called pacanes."

Pacanes, in fact, was the American Indian word for all hard-to-crack nuts. In translation pecan became the common term used by all French-speaking settlers living in the Mississippi basin.

The pecan is a hickory, and both are in the same family as walnuts but not of the same genus. Native pecan trees grow in greatest numbers in Texas, Oklahoma, Arkansas, Louisiana, and Mississippi.

The largest crops from wild and cultivated pecan trees come from those states and six others—Georgia, Alabama, New Mexico, North and South Carolina, and Florida. The range of pecan trees is being expanded by experiments in other parts of the country.

Pecan trees in America are "more important than native fruit plants of any other kind . . ." according to a treatise written by three horticulturists. The tall trees produce hundreds of millions of nuts a year, provide shade for lawns, and hardwood for flooring, furniture veneer, wall paneling, and for shafts of golf clubs, hammers, and axes. Cultivated trees produce millions more pounds of edible nuts.

It is claimed the oval-shaped pecan is the second most popular nut in the United States, the peanut being first. Salted pecans are a delicacy, and the natural nuts are particularly enjoyed when ingredients of pecan pie, butter pecan ice cream, and of the praline—a brown sugar candy of French origin.

Only ten to fifteen percent of marketed pecans are in-shell; all others are shelled. In every pound of the shelled pecans, there are 3633 calories. One fully developed kernel has a content of about seventy percent oil, almost all of it unsaturated.

The rich, nourishing pecans come from self-fertile trees, but commercial orchards usually are planted with pollinizer species for cross-fertilization. Pollen is chiefly wind distributed.

Female flowers bloom in the year they are pollinated. Male flowers begin to develop nearly a year before they produce pollen. The male flowers on one spray, or catkin, may contain more than 2.5 million grains of pollen. Fifty thousand pounds of pecans can develop from that much pollen, on the basis of one grain for one pecan.

Vegetative propagation for cultivated pecans is done by budding and grafting. Native trees are often topworked.

A few nuts develop on most cultivated trees by age three or four. Mature crops are harvested any time between the seventh and tenth year, depending on the species and management of the grove. The pounds of nuts harvested increase with the age of a tree. A tree may yield fifty pounds per year from ages ten to fifteen, and from seventy-five to 100 pounds from ages fifteen to twenty.

Pecan tree.

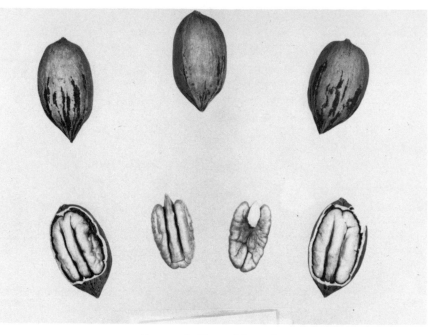

Pecan shells and kernels.

There are continuing experiments with cultivated pecan trees. Among other hoped-for results are disease and pest control, improved methods of orchard care and harvesting, and, of course, crop increases.

No matter how successful the horticultural programs are, it is unlikely that any cultivated pecan tree will ever match the crop record of one native pecan tree in Bell County, Texas.

The Texas pecan, 125 feet tall, with a limb spread of 100 feet, and a trunk diameter of forty inches, was named No. 735 the year it produced 735 pounds of nuts. Its annual crops previously, for many years, varied from 400 to 500 pounds. No. 735 outdid itself, in 1954, by producing 1000 pounds of pecans.

10

CHESTNUTS

A dreadful disease killed millions of American chestnut trees in only four decades, from about 1900 to 1940.

American chestnut trees for centuries grew wild in open country and up mountain slopes of eastern North America. The range of the tree was east of the Appalachian Mountains and from southern Quebec Province into what is now the Deep South of the United States.

The large trees grew to 100 feet and had huge leaf spreads. Trunks, or stems, were three feet or more in circumference. Lumber was used for fence posts; for beams of barns and houses, and, in railroad construction, for the ties across tracks, under the rails.

From the late eighteenth century through the nineteenth, American chestnuts were popular planting trees. They lined country roads and town streets, beautified lawns and parks.

Two to three nuts in thin brown shells formed inside the green chestnut burs, covered with bristles. The nut kernels were a major food for many kinds of wildlife. People enjoyed the delicious flavor of chestnuts in stews and in turkey dressing. They roasted chestnuts in ovens, in fireplace grates, and over

Burs and nuts of Chinese chestnut.

campfires. Street vendors, in big cities, sold bags of hot chestnuts, fresh roasted on small carts set against sidewalk curbs.

Just before 1900 a number of diseased chestnut trees from the Far East were planted in the United States. A fungus of the foreign trees attacked the bark of American chestnuts. The disease girdled, or circled, tree trunks, rotted the bark, and killed the trees.

The first seriously damaged American chestnuts were found in a Long Island grove, near New York City. Through study of those trees, the disease was identified as Asian. Sometimes known as chestnut-bark disease and chestnut canker, it is commonly called chestnut blight. The blight rapidly spread from Long Island, through New York State, and then fanned up and down the whole region where American chestnuts grew.

Efforts to control the disease, to cure the trees, completely failed. The American chestnut, such fun to roast, so sweet to eat, was almost extinct by 1940. A few of the trees, not native to northern California and the Pacific Northwest, grow there and are free from chestnut blight.

In the East thousands of leafless trees, killed by the blight were cut down. Countless others toppled over in forests. Fallen and rotting logs of American chestnuts are a source of tannin, the same chemical compound taken from acorns and from black oak bark.

Wildlife suffered most from the killing of American chest-

Chinese chestnut trees in Allegheny National Forest, Pennsylvania.

nuts. Many animal and bird species were reduced in numbers for lack of food. The wild turkey disappeared from certain areas, including western Virginia.

There are many new plantings of chestnuts for wildlife. Various blight-resistant varieties are grown on game preserves.

Millions of pounds of European chestnuts have been exported to the United States since 1940. But European chestnuts transplanted on the East Coast are ruined by the blight. Even in Europe the trees are increasingly damaged by chestnut blight and by a root fungus called the ink disease.

For good reason chestnut blight does not attack horse chestnut trees. They do not belong to the same family as the diseased chestnuts.

Horse chestnuts, shipped to the west from Turkey in the sixteenth century, flourish in temperate zones of the world. The well-shaped trees are planted for shade, not for their nut crops. The nut kernels are inedible unless treated by complicated techniques.

Certain tribes of American Indians knew how to prepare and cook the kernels from one small variety called the buckeye. The nickname of Ohio is the Buckeye State because so many trees of that horse chestnut variety grow there.

The beautiful shells of some varieties of horse chestnut are as large as those of Persian walnuts. Shells are reddish brown, shiny, and smooth to touch. They make great playthings for small children.

There are various superstitions and tall tales about the horse chestnut. People carry one as a good luck charm, or to keep from having the aches and pains of rheumatism or arthritis. Horses are supposed to have been given the nuts as food or as medicine. Dogs are said to search for a horse chestnut to chew, when sick. Various horse chestnut cures for human illnesses have been suggested.

In the United States the horse chestnut remains a popular ornamental. It is not likely to be widely used for medicine or for food.

Nuts of blight-resistant true chestnuts already provide food for wildlife and people. Chestnuts dry out fast if not promptly and properly cured, so processing methods are important. Curing also makes the nuts more nutritious because it changes their heavy starch content to sugar. Botanists continue to experiment with and to develop chestnut varieties for American food of the future.

11

FILBERT (HAZELNUT)

Pliny, the Roman naturalist, wrote in A.D. 60, "Filberts and hazels . . . are a kind of nut. . . ." Nuts from the trees of the genus *Corylus* are known today as filberts and/or hazelnuts.

Early writings refer to the magic of hazelnuts and hazelwood. According to legend hazelnuts were burned on ancient altars to help priests predict the future. The first divining rods, or dowsers, were forked twigs of hazelwood.

Similar to the forked almond twigs of Tuscan treasure hunters in Italy, hazelwood divining rods were tools for locating both minerals and water underground. The forked twigs, held in horizontal position, automatically pointed down, it was said, when ore or water was beneath the surface of the ground.

A folk superstition of Cornwall, a county in England, tells of pixies, or little people, who guided hazelwood divining rods. If those holding the rods were not in favor with the pixies, the little people interfered with the search. They supposedly either kept the forked sticks from moving out of the horizontal position or directed them to wrong locations.

The origin of the name filbert for the nuts from hazel trees is confused in history. Some sources say the nuts were nicknamed "full beard" for fringed husks completely covering the shells of some species. The husks do look like long bushy beards. Others claim the name comes from Saint Philibert whose special day in August coincides with the ripening of the first nuts of the yearly crop in England.

Filberts and hazelnuts sold in world markets are grown chiefly in Europe, Central Asia, and North Africa. Less than ten percent are cultivated in the United States, principally in the Pacific Northwest.

Native North American hazel trees grow from Maine west to Saskatchewan and south to Georgia, Missouri, and Oklahoma. Very few of the native nuts are marketed. American hazelnuts,

"Full Beard" husk of the Barcelona variety of filbert.

primarily harvested for use by local people, also provide food for wildlife.

The species commercially grown in the United States are European, not native, filberts. Oregon produces more than ninety percent of the commercial American crop, and the state of Washington, less than five percent.

The first European filbert species were planted in Nevada City, California, in 1885, by Felix Gillet, a nurseryman. For twenty years he experimented with numerous species, many of them now cultivated in the Northwest. Filbert cultivation in California was not continued. Climate is suitable in the Willamette Valley of Oregon, and in a small area of Washington.

Plants of the genus *Corylus* grow naturally as bushes or as shrubby trees with several trunks. Heights are about ten feet. In Oregon the European species, from fifteen to twenty-five feet high, have single trunks. The single trunk is attained by re-

Orchard of cultivated filberts with single trunks.

Filbert kernels.

moval of suckers, or shoots, from around a central stem. If permitted to develop, the suckers become additional trunks.

Suckering, or removing the shoots, is a continuing process in filbert orchards. Suckers are plentiful around the base of new growth, and removal of shoots from around new trees is an important operation. Some suckering is required even after the central trunks are woody and mature.

A filbert tree has both male and female flowers but is not self-fertile. Orchards are planted with selected pollinizers in various numbers, depending on the species. Full crops of nuts are harvested by the time trees are six years old.

Ripe filberts fall out of their husks and onto the ground in late September or early October. Shells and their kernels are shaped like either a cone or ball. Small round kernels are the preference of the principal buyers—candy manufacturers and bakers.

71

Layering is the method commonly used for vegetative propagation of filberts. Sometimes a sucker of a tree is curved down for rooting in the soil. More often a root or stump, called a stool, is bent S-shape with a tip end standing up and one bend in the earth for rooting. Layering, done in the spring, produces a root section by fall. The new growth is then cut loose from the main stem tree, or from the root or stump placed in what is known as the stoolbed.

Pomologists are trying to find a rootstock for the satisfactory grafting or budding of filberts in the future.

12

COCONUT

Everything about the coconut palm is extraordinary. Its hard-shelled fruit floats. The smooth gray trunk does not increase in girth as it grows in height. There is one seed, and it develops as a plant inside the shell.

The leaves, buds, flowers, and meat surrounding the seed of the palm variously provide people with food, drink, and clothes; with household furnishings and utensils; with materials for construction; with quantities of valuable oil; with jobs and income from commercial sales.

The origin of coconuts is a mystery not yet solved. How coconuts reached the places where they now grow is well known.

Travelers, from ancient times, transported coconuts from country to country in caravans and on ships, often as ballast. But most coconuts floated to new locales, down rivers and across oceans.

A ripe coconut is buoyant, and its husk is waterproofed by a natural wax coating. A coconut, fallen from a palm into water, will bob along until it is beached on a shoreline, close-by or thousands of miles away.

The coconut palm is old. It goes back in history to Sanskrit records of more than 3000 years ago. An Egyptian, in 545 B.C., called the palm's fruit the "great Nut of India." Marco Polo, the Venetian traveler, saw the palms in Sumatra in the late thirteenth century A.D. In 1577 English navigator Sir Francis Drake described coconuts of the Cape Verde Islands as "no lesse goode and sweete than almonds."

Today major crops of coconuts come from Malaya, Indonesia, the southwest Pacific islands, Ceylon, and the Philippines.

In the Western Hemisphere coconut palms grow in very humid areas of some islands, of Central America, of Mexico, and Florida. The Florida palms are chiefly ornamental and, in the few sections where they will grow, do not fruit regularly or abundantly.

The first coconut palms in Florida probably sprouted from waterborne coconuts. Many palms were raised after a Spanish ship, carrying a cargo of coconuts, was wrecked in 1878 off the east coast of Florida, just south of Palm Beach.

Salvaged coconuts produced nearly 350,000 palms. But, after cold and frost wiped out most of the palms in a single season, plans for development of a coconut industry in Florida were scrapped.

The bulk of the American supply of coconuts is imported from the Philippines.

Coconut palms may be from seventy to one hundred feet high. Their trunks, without branches, are almost never straight, because they curve themselves. When several trees are no more than six to eight feet apart at the base, the trunks bend away from each other. Trunks of palms near an ocean beach or on a river bank lean toward the water.

OPPOSITE: *Ripe coconuts on the palm tree.*

Instead of one strong root the coconut palm has 4000 to 8000 slender roots spreading out from the tree base for distances from fifteen feet to thirty; some roots go underground for fifty feet. The root system not only draws up large quantities of water for the tree, but also is a protective anchor for it during hurricanes and typhoons.

Flowers, yellow or white, at the top of the coconut palm are almost hidden by its large crown of thirty to forty feathery leaves. Pollinization is chiefly by insects, sometimes by wind. The fruit develops in three months after flowering and ripens in about ten months.

Coconut fruit consists of a green outer husk, covered with fibers; a hard brown shell; the white meat kernel; a liquid, the coconut milk; and the single seed.

A germinated seed is kept moist by the milk and is nourished

Coconut meat inside husk with heavy fibers.

by the same coconut meat we eat. The developed plant from the seed penetrates the shell and sprouts through a soft spot in the husk.

The husk is important, in nature and commerce. Milk from young coconuts is drawn through the same soft spot the sprout breaks through. If a fruit falls to the ground, the fibrous husk acts as a cushion to prevent damage to the shell. After harvest, husk fibers are used for products woven by hand and machine.

Cultivated trees will bear in seven to ten years, produce mature crops from fifteen to fifty, and continue to bear up to seventy. Like citrus trees coconut palms bloom and fruit year-round. In some years a palm may bear 200 coconuts, but a good annual harvest is sixty coconuts per tree. On commercial plantations in the Philippines, coconuts are harvested every two months, or ten at a time from each tree. The clusters are removed by sickle-shaped knives attached to long bamboo poles.

Workers, mostly women, equipped with pointed sticks, gather harvested coconuts into piles for pickup. Water buffalo pull sleds filled with coconuts to the husking area and processing plant.

The husking device has a clawlike base fixed firmly to the ground. Above is a metal cylinder supporting a long spike, sharp as a sword. Skilled and strong men jam the coconuts onto the spikes to remove the husks. The men wear protective leather cuffs, up to the elbows, and leather aprons over leg coverings similar to cowboy chaps.

Most of the processing of shelling and paring is done by hand labor.

On an eight-hour shift one man can crack and shell 1600 to 1800 coconuts. A full crew is capable of stripping 800,000 coconuts in one day.

Women remove the skin from meat kernels with specially

designed paring knives. Stationed side by side along conveyor lines, women inspectors examine pared and washed coconuts en route to mechanical shredders.

The machines turn out chips, flakes, and threads, or shredded coconuts, and various grinds from coarse to extra fine. Afterwards the prepared coconut is dried in narrow ovens longer than bowling alleys.

Dried coconut, in its various forms, is sold in world markets for baking cakes, sweet rolls, pies, macaroons and other cookies; for making candy, ambrosia, and dessert puddings. Relatively few coconuts are shipped in-shell for retail customers.

Shells and husks are not discarded. The shells are made into cups, ladles, bowls, and other objects, both decorative and useful. Fibers of the husk, which make good furniture stuffing, are woven into floor mats and cordage, the rope of marine lines for boats and docks.

Oil is a major coconut product. The liquid, pressed from dried coconuts, or copra, is an ingredient in some kinds of soap, shaving cream, shampoo, cotton dye, candles, ointments, and cosmetics. Coconut oil, in liquid state, has been a cooking oil for thousands of years; in semisolid state, it is a substitute for lard.

Natives hand-carve and hand-weave coconut products for their homes and their trades. They make salads with tender flower stems and the coconut bud, called palm cabbage. The meat kernel is eaten ripe or not, cooked or uncooked.

Liquid from the flowers is drunk fresh, like fruit juice, or is distilled for vinegar and the alcoholic beverage, palm wine, or palm toddy.

Leaf ribs and the whole leaves, often eighteen feet long, are made into brooms, brushes, fans, hats, thatch for roofs, and baskets for marketing and home storage. Buildings in the tropics are constructed of coconut lumber.

Some experts say the coconut is not only the most important palm in the world but the most useful tree. Its by-products and food tonnage are on the increase, and so is its importance to the economy of several regions.

In the Philippines 273 million coconut palms are planted on 4.5 million acres of land. The trees produce nearly 9 billion coconuts a year. The number annually harvested worldwide is between 15 billion and 18 billion.

13

CASHEW

Cashew nuts come from an odd tree. It bears two fruits and produces a black juice that is both poisonous and medicinal.

Cashew trees originated in tropic regions of Brazil. They are now native in other parts of South America, in Central America and the West Indies, in Africa and Asia.

Major commercial crops are harvested in East Africa and India. The cultivated trees are thirty to forty feet high and very beautiful, with spreading evergreen branches. The leaves are round and notched at the top; rose-colored flowers give off a fragrant scent.

Some varieties of cashew trees are small and without full foliage. Those grown in southern Florida, only as interesting specimens, are neither ornamental nor full bearing.

Cashew trees are fast growing. The fruit ripens in three to four months after the blossoming. Seeds germinate in a month or less, and trees, fully matured, bear good crops at four to five years.

The real fruit, the inch-long nut in a double shell, is shiny, grayish in color, and shaped like a kidney. The other fruit, botanically known as the receptacle, is really a very large bulbous stalk. Although it is shaped like a pear, the edible receptacle is called the cashew apple or, occasionally, the mahogany apple. It is juicy, slightly sour, and, when mature, red or yellow, depending on the variety. The nut develops at the big end of the three-inch cashew apple, and sticks out from it like a plump stem.

There is black juice, a bitter, poisonous oil, between the inner and outer shells of the nut. On contact with human skin the oil blisters and causes peeling, like poison ivy.

Before shelling, the cashew is roasted for removal of the acrid oil. Precautions are taken during the roasting because smoke from the heated nuts severely irritates the eyes, and causes painful swelling of the skin. The fumes can make people very ill, sometimes fatally.

Cashew nut tree in East Africa.

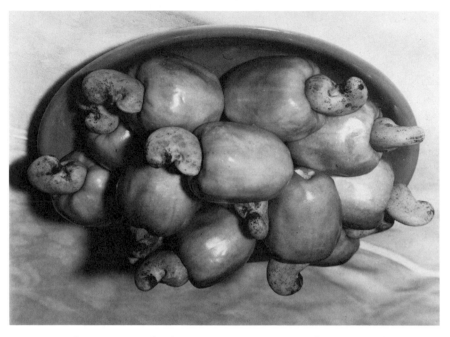

Cashew nuts in shell growing out of receptacle, also edible.

The caustic oil is also in the bark and the sap of the tree. The black juice and a milky substance from under the bark are combined for the indelible marking of laundry. The sap is made into varnish for the protection of woodwork and leather-bound books against insect damage. As resin it is useful in the manufacture of electrical appliances.

Natives apply the sap as medicinal gum and, in some locales, treat leprosy with oil extracted directly from the shells. A medicine from the tree bark is given to malaria patients allergic to quinine, the standard cure for that fever. West Indians remove warts and corns with the black juice, and use it for treatment of two serious diseases—ringworm and elephantiasis.

Cashew apple jam is a delicacy, and the fruit is eaten raw

wherever it is native, but it is not exported. The juice is regionally fermented as wine.

Light-colored oil, pressed out of the roasted nut kernel, is very much like olive oil and similarly used for cooking and salad dressing. The oil is added as flavor to various wines, including the famous Madeira.

The delicious rich-tasting cashew was not widely known until much later than many nuts. After introduction to foreign markets, the cashew became commercially successful as one American statistic indicates. In the years between 1929 and 1940, the export tonnage of cashew nuts from India to the United States increased by 622 percent.

The cashew, roasted and salted, is steadily gaining worldwide popularity.

14

PEANUT

Peanuts are not nuts. They are legumes related to peas and lima and other beans. But peanuts differ from the pod vegetables by developing and maturing underground.

The peanut vine grows as a small bush about a foot and a half high, or trails along the ground. Peanut varieties of the first type are bunch plants, the second are called Runners.

After the self-pollinating yellow flowers fade and die, a peg forms on the vine. The peg, or fruit stem, buries itself two to three inches underground, and the pod develops in horizontal position.

Most varieties have two seeds to the pod, or shell. The heart, or embryo, is a nugget, meaty as the peanut, nestled between the halves of each split seed. Seeds are covered with a red skin. Peanut varieties mature from 120 days, the earliest, to more than twenty weeks, for the latest.

The peanut originated in South America, where it is called *maní*. From excavated objects archaeologists know pre-Columbian Indians cultivated peanuts. Among the unearthed finds are peanut-shaped bowls, pottery decorated with peanut de-

ABOVE: *Peanuts of bunch plant crop uprooted by diggers at harvest time.*

BELOW: *Peanuts, shelled and in shell.*

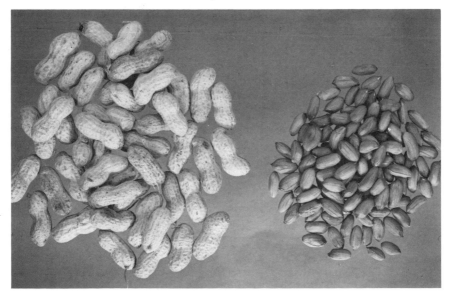

signs, and, from ancient tombs, utensils filled with peanuts very much like those grown in modern Peru.

Spanish conquistadors returned home with peanuts from Peru; and seeds from plantings in Spain were traded with Africans. The peanut flourished in Africa and became staple food.

Many natives worshipped the peanut, along with other plants supposed to have souls, like human beings. According to legend gold peanuts hammered from crude ore were trophies of the sixteenth century in Africa. Tribal chieftains presented the gold peanuts to warriors, athletes, and hunters.

Africans, sold in slavery to owners in Virginia, planted peanuts left over from the food supplies of slave ships. The vines, sprouting around plantation huts in an American colony, reminded the slaves of their homeland and native customs.

Slaves from Angola called peanuts goobers. Goober and goober peas, common terms for peanuts in colonial America, are still familiar in Southern parts of the United States. Other nicknames are groundnut, ground pea, and earthnut.

Mpinda, the word for peanut in the Congo, is translated to *pinda* in English but is used only in the West Indies.

For many years Southerners scorned goober peas as food fit only for poor folks, slaves, and hogs. Then a few farmers who liked the taste of the peanut began to plant a couple of rows in truck gardens, along with tomatoes, turnips, corn, onions, and potatoes.

After the Civil War peanuts were taken north in the pockets of Union soldiers. They had acquired a taste for the goober peas eaten in great quantities by Confederate forces.

Peanuts were introduced to more Americans by traveling circuses and at baseball stadiums. Circus hawkers sold roasted peanuts for customers to eat in the stands and to feed animals of the menagerie, particularly elephants. Butcher boys carried small bags of peanuts for sale to fans in bleachers at ball parks.

George Washington Carver, director of agricultural research at Tuskegee Institute in Alabama, began peanut experiments in 1897. The distinguished black scientist was internationally recognized for various achievements, but none was more remarkable than his contribution to the peanut industry of the United States.

He advised on improvement of peanut crops and made possible 300 ways to use peanuts, their shells, and plants.

Dr. Carver extracted thirty dyes from peanut skins and devised a material of peanut shells and other substances for the manufacture of wallboard. Leather stains, wood stains, and ink evolved from his research laboratory. It was difficult to tell the difference between his peanut curds and ground meat. From peanuts he also made instant coffee and instant cream; skimmed milk, called blue John in Alabama; evaporated milk and buttermilk; cream for making ice cream; and a condiment sauce, like Worcestershire.

Dr. Carver was responsible for a large increase in commercial crops of peanuts in Alabama and, indirectly, elsewhere. A whole county in Alabama was about to be bankrupt after boll weevil blight wiped out cotton crops. Dr. Carver, a pioneer ecologist, suggested peanut crops, not only as a source of income in place of cotton, but for enriching the soil.

His plan worked, and growers made more profit from peanuts than they ever had from cotton. The town of Enterprise even erected a statue to the boll weevil, the beetle pest, not to the money-making peanuts.

The success of growers in Alabama encouraged farmers in other states to plant more acres of peanuts. In addition to Alabama and Virginia, the states now producing major peanut crops are Georgia, Texas, Florida, North Carolina, Oklahoma,

Mississippi, and New Mexico. But the United States produces less than ten percent commercially grown peanuts of the world.

India, China, and West Africa, leaders in the cultivation of peanuts, export almost their entire crops. Few peanuts are eaten in those countries.

Western Europe imports peanuts and processes peanut oil for which there is great demand in many countries. The peanut meat left over when the oil is all crushed out is called peanut meal. It is sold as feed for poultry and livestock.

Oil and the meal are exported from the United States, but the bulk of the American crop is for edible peanut products. Only about a third of the crop is put to other uses.

Peanuts are harvested by hand everywhere except in the United States where mechanical diggers cut the main root, lift the plants, and shake loose the dirt.

For natural drying, vines are either spread along the ground, or draped on poles, like so many small haystacks. Field drying is preferred by many growers, but mechanical drying bins and wagon driers are also used. Picking is totally mechanical.

Peanut hay for livestock feed is a valuable by-product of the harvest. Following the harvest many growers run hogs out into the cleared fields to feed on any peanuts dropped or missed by the machines. Some crops are raised just for "hogging-in."

In the processing plants, peanuts are cleaned, sorted to size, and those to be sold in-shell separated for roasting. Shelled peanuts are skinned by various kinds of rubbing machines. The red skins are rubbed off by revolving fine hair brushes, or by ribbed rubber belting, or vibrating pads covered with canvas.

After further sorting and final inspection, shelled peanuts are shipped from the plant.

Among present-day by-products of the peanut industry are such nonfoods as shaving cream, adhesives, paper, plastics, salve,

Red skins removed from peanut kernels by vibrating pad.

cosmetics, shoe polish, metal polish, ink, dyes, lubricating oils, and fertilizer. Products just from the shells include insulation filler, buffing for steel mills, floor sweeping compounds, carriers for certain kinds of deactivated chemicals, and wallboard.

Oil, extracted from whole peanuts, the skins and the hearts removed from kernels, is refined for various uses. It is a cooking and salad oil and an ingredient for cheese, mayonnaise, and margarine.

Edible peanuts produced in the United States are sold in-shell, five percent; for candy, twenty percent; salted, twenty-five percent; and for the manufacture of peanut butter, fifty percent.

Peanut butter was first made in 1890 by a doctor in St. Louis, Missouri. Trying to find a high protein food for certain patients, he beat up a batch of peanut paste. The "butter" was easy to digest, nutritious, and appetizing. Friends and relatives of the invalids dipped into the mixture and liked it. Peanut butter for years after was homemade, and then, following World War I, gained popularity as a manufactured product.

No one knows who invented the peanut butter and jelly sandwich.

New inventions of high protein peanut foods were announced in 1973 at two universities—Clemson and Florida. J. H. Mitchell, Jr., professor of food science in Clemson's College of Agricultural Sciences, introduced peanut flakes. The flakes are slice kernels. They can be made into cereal, dry or to-be-cooked, and into lunch meat that is two-thirds flake and one-third meat or fowl.

At the University of Florida, Dr. Esam Ahmed and his colleagues made standard food dishes from peanut grits, a substance with oil extracted. The grits have been cooked as meatballs and, with the addition of an egg yolk, as hamburger substitute. The latter is named Samburger for Dr. E*sam* Ahmed.

In the Far East and Africa, where most peanuts are commercially grown, many adults and children are undernourished; some starve to death. Perhaps peanut butter, peanut flakes, and peanut grits will one day be food staples in those countries.

SUGGESTED READING

HANDBOOK OF NORTH AMERICAN NUT TREES, Richard A. Jaynes, Editor, The North American Nut Growers Association

FRUIT AND NUT GROWING, Boy Scouts of America

INDEX

Italic numbers refer to illustrations.

cashews, 80–83, *81*, *82*
Central America, 74, 80
Central Valley, California, 33, 52
Ceylon, 74
cherries, 17
chestnut-bark disease, 64
chestnuts, 17
   American, 63–65
   Chinese, *64*, *65*
   European, 14, 66
chestnuts, horse, *see* horse chestnuts
Chico, California, 34
Chile, 52
China, 27, 88
Chinese-layering, 30
Chios, Greece, 35
chipmunks, 11
Civil War, U.S., 11, 14, 57–58, 86
cleaners, commercial, 37, 57, 89
Clemson University, 90
climate, 27, 33, 42, 46–47, 51–52, 66,
   70, 74, 80
coconuts, 17, 73–79, *75*, *76*
coffee substitutes, 14, 87
Congo, 86
copra, 78
corns, 82
Cornwall, England, 68
Correggio, Antonio, 57
Corylus (hazelnut) species, 68, 70
cosmetics, 32, 44, 78, 89
Costa Rica, 50
cotton, 34, 87
crows, 11, 21

deer, 23
   white-tailed, 11
diabetes, 44
Diamond Walnut Growers, Inc., 52, 57
diseases, plant, 31, 34, 42, 50, 62, 63–67
divining rods, 40, 68
dogs, 66
dowsers (divining rods), 40, 68
Drake, Sir Francis, 74
Druids, 13
drupe, definition of, 17
dyes, 16, 57–58, 78, 87, 89

earthnuts, 86
ecology, 87
elephantiasis, 82
endocarp (drupe section), 17–18, 37
England, 68–69

epicarp (drupe section), 17–18, 37
Europe, 32, 40, 69, 88
Everett, David, 13

feed, livestock, 11, 23, 37, 44, 57, 88
fertilizers, 20, 34, 42, 57, 89
filberts, *see* hazelnuts
firebricks, 57
flooring, 57
Florida, 29, 49–50, 59, 80, 87
Florida, University of, 90
flowers:
   female, 18, 35, 53–54, 71
   male, 18, 35, 53–54, 71
   perfect, 18, 47
Fowler, W. D., 34–37
Fresno, California, 35
fruit, definition of, 17
fungus, shot-hole, 42

Gaul (France), 13
Georgia, 59, 69, 87
germination, 14, 20–21
Gillet, Felix, 70
goobers, 86
grafting, 18–20, 60
grapes, Muscat, 29–30, 56
Greece, 13, 32, 40
groundnuts, 86
ground peas, 86
Gympie, Australia, 45
gympie nuts, 45

harvesting, commercial, 23, 37, 44, 49,
   54, *55*, 62, 77, 88
Hawaii, University of, 50
Hawaiian Islands, 27, 46–50
Hawaii island, 47
Hawaii State Department of Agriculture,
   47
hazelnuts (filberts), 17, 68–72
   American, 69
   European, 69, *69*, 70, *71*
headaches, 58
heaters, plant, 42–43
heights, tree, 13, 24, 29, 33, 47, 53, 63,
   70, 74, 80
hickory nuts, 59
Hilo, Hawaii, 49
horse chestnuts, 66–67
horses, 66
horticulture, 16, 34, 59
hull rot disease, 42

93

771105M

634
POO

Poole, Gray Johnson

Nuts from forest,
orchard, and field

634
POO

Poole, Gray Johnson   771105M

Nuts from forest,
orchard, and field

DATE	BORROWER'S NAME	
NOV. 15.	Dani Allens-v	